SLOP
Essays Against AI

Cover design by Annabel Townsend

First Printing, 2026
The Wanderings Series is an imprint of Pete's Press

Slop

Essays against AI

With contributions from:
Annabel Townsend, The Real Flydog, S. Portico Bowman, Kai Hutchence, John Klein and Andrea Martineau

THE WANDERINGS SERIES

*Dedicated to all the creative, messy, fallible,
perfectly-imperfect humans still out there.*

Contents

1

I Just Don't Get It.

By Annabel Townsend

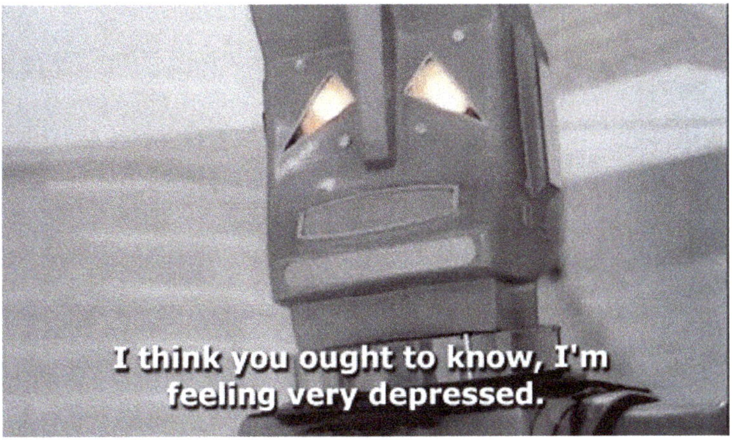

Marvin the depressed robot from Hitchhiker's Guide to the Galaxy by Douglas Adams

Douglas Adams had an interesting idea when he created the character of Marvin the depressed robot in *Hitchhikers' Guide to the Galaxy.* If you invented a machine that had access to, and understood, the sum total of all human knowledge, the chances are it would indeed end up very depressed. We've gotten very close to this already. We don't yet have robots like Marvin, but we have created AI machines that could potentially contain the world's knowledge. But instead of becoming depressed, the AI bots are making people like me depressed.

Like it or not, machine-learning and Large Language Models (LLMs) have infiltrated our lives already. It has fundamentally changed the way we work, the way we use the internet, the way we write and sometimes even the way we think. At the time of writing this essay, we can still avoid it - refuse to use it, and not buy into the hype. AI is still optional, but it may not be for long. The fact remains that we cannot 'un-invent' it. But just because we *can* do something, does not mean we *should*.

I asked – no, *prompted* — ChatGPT to write the opening paragraph for me:

> "Artificial intelligence is transforming the way we approach writing, particularly in academic and professional settings. The advent of AI-powered writing tools has made it easier than ever to generate essays, create polished drafts, and refine com-plex arguments. While AI can streamline the writing process and enhance creativity by generating ideas or suggesting improvements, it also raises questions about originality, ethics, and the value of human insight in writing. As AI increasingly becomes part of academic and creative endeavors, it challenges traditional notions of authorship and compels us to reconsider what it means to write authentically."

I suspect this introduction is going to rot in literary purgatory, neglected and unseen. That is far from an attention-grabbing paragraph! For anyone who hasn't immediately switched off – please bear with me and read on. I promise there is more soul and humanity in later paragraphs.

Credit where credit is due, that ChatGPT paragraph does at least admit that machine-generated content is problematic. I am more amazed that it didn't use the phrases "the labyrinth of possibilities" or "the rich tapestry of…", did not invite us to "embark on a journey" or 'delve into' something, and did not describe anything as 'captivating'.

It's not just generic - it's repetitive. It doesn't just bore you - it amplifies the lack of creativity. And the kicker? There's no way to stop it.

Play with the tech enough, and you start to recognise AI-generated writing when you come across it. *Know your enemy.* I am no expert in ChatGPT, but I deliberately made time to familiarize myself with it. It is my job to read critically, after all. I also wanted to know what to look for when vetting potential authors and freelancers at my publishing business. I do this, because I've already been burned by it.

Earlier in the year, I commissioned a freelance copyeditor that I'd been working with for a while already, to write a blurb for the back of a book. A small job, and mercifully not too costly. When I received his 'work' back, I didn't like it much – lots of unnecessarily complicated language, repetition and it somehow didn't sound like *him.* I figured he was just having an off day, or he hadn't much liked the book in question. Not the end of the world, and I dismissed my concerns. He'd fulfilled the job and met the deadline, so I paid up anyway. I just wasted more of my time reworking it before I could use it. More fool me. Of course I can't fully prove it, but since I started messing with AI, I am about 90% confident he simply wrote "write a back cover blurb for a book about…." into ChatGPT and copied and pasted its response to me. This is *not* what I paid him for.

I understand that using ChatGPT saves you time, that it can act as 'inspiration' for your own real creativity, and that for some tasks, it can make life a little easier. But without those pressures, I do not understand why anyone would want to use it for anything creative, let alone use it and try to pass it off as their own work. S. Portico Bowman examines AI's effects on creative work in her article in Chapter Four.

Another incident passed my way recently. This time, I was copyediting a collaborative document that formed part of a bid for a large and lucrative contract for a project management company. The bid had been passed around a fair bit before I saw it, and I read the others' comments to get myself up to speed. They were suggesting using ChatGPT to rewrite sections that they weren't confident about. Knowing these folks are not writers, and that they had other priorities besides creating sharp, persuasive copy, I can understand the motivation to do so.

But what about their competitors?

If this company thinks to use ChatGPT to write their bids, there's a high chance that their competitors would do the same. And given the remit is the same for every company bidding, the prompt they plug into ChatGPT would also be very similar. This is only going to result in their bid being nearly identical to their competitors', and that does no one any favours.

From Redditor : GrobTheory

For the sake of this post, I will call it ChatGPT as that is the platform I have experienced, but I know there are other competing companies doing the same thing. I do not like to call it 'Artificial Intelligence'. It is not, and never will be "intelligent." At best, it is 'Machine learning' or modelling. At worst, it is plagiarism software, nothing more.

There is an argument to be made that this form of machine learning is 'just a tool', like using the preset paint brushes in Photoshop, or using a spellchecker to find my typos. "The artist designs the prompts for the machine to use" sounds safe and reassuring, as if the human artist is still involved. But there is a big, big difference. Assistive 'AI' is a tool – the spellcheck, the colour fill option and so on – but *generative* AI is where it all comes crashing down.

Generative 'AI' is using other people's words to generate copy from a machine. It's like using a robotic knitting machine to make a sweater, stealing the pattern from someone, stealing the yarn from someone else, and then labelling it 'handmade' because a human hand programmed the pattern into it and pressed the On switch.

I call it 'machine learning' because it does 'learn' – but it learns to copy, never to create. It learns through repetition and data storage – rote-learning. It puts me in mind of my physics classes in high school: you could pass the class if you just memorised the formula. We were taught just enough to pass the exams, but there was little need for real understanding of the topics. In the same manner, ChatGPT regurgitates just enough to appear 'intelligent' but has no real understanding of what it produces.

If rehashed text produced at high speed is what you require, then so be it – but I urge you to consider the other, worse, elements of generative AI use:

The words it 'learns' from have to come from somewhere — and for the moment, that is from unknowing, uncredited humans.

ChatGPT and the other bots scrape the entire internet to feed their machine, and it will steal work and repackage it for you, for free, while the original creators find it harder and harder to find decent work. US publishers and authors have already successfully sued AI company, Anthropic, over the theft of thousands of published books to train their LLM, and more lawsuits are being filed all the time.

I am regularly scrolling LinkedIn's job recommendations for anything 'writer'-related at the moment, and it is mightily depressing. There are so many ads for "AI Prompt Writers" – companies actually trying to hire writers to help make their own industry obsolete. It's like trying to hire authors to work in a book pulping company. If all this wasn't bad enough, there is a growing body of evidence that suggests, aside from stealing the work from writers and artists, using AI frequently for every little thing - writing emails to research to recipe suggestions - actually impairs your cognitive function.(1) The brain is like any other muscle; use it or lose it. If we outsource our thinking to AI, we run the risk of cognitive atrophy. Kai Hutchence uncovers the effects of AI in education in the next chapter.

In turn, losing our critical thinking skills may even benefit AI companies. If we can no longer tell what is real and what is generated by AI, and if we no longer have the skills to even question the media we're consuming, we are much less equipped to fight against it. Knowledge is power, and this is straight out of a dystopian novel.

LinkedIn remains infuriating in many respects, but recently it is too full of gen-AI posts. A friend of mine who works in tech -though I've no idea in what capacity -is also putting herself though university online. She posted a poll asking how often her network uses ChatGPT? A concerning number voted "Daily". My friend went on to say how she fed her university journal articles into ChatGPT and got it to summarize them for her, like making crib notes. My initial reaction was "What happened to 'reading for a degree'?" But then I thought about it more carefully.

Those journal articles are copyrighted.

Either to the author/researcher who wrote the paper, or to the university, or more likely, to the academic publisher. My friend can only access the journals because she's signed up for her degree course. They are not publicly available otherwise, and certainly not free.

But by copy-and-pasting the whole thing into ChatGPT, she is inadvertently posting the author's work into the public domain. Not overtly, but ChatGPT will store it indefinitely and then mine it for information for anyone else who uses a similar prompt. And there is no way to stop it, no way of removing the information, and no credit nor royalties going to its author.

(When I pointed this out to her, she deleted my comment, too.)

I am aware that this is 'freeing up academia!' and making knowledge accessible to everyone! And fun stuff like that. I agree – but if you really want to make education accessible to all, then get rid of tuition fees and forgive student debt. Don't screw over the academics who bothered to do the reading and researching by themselves by denying them credit for their work.

Another consequence of letting machine learning scrape its sources from the internet is the biases it then 'learns' from our already problematic content. Most people are familiar with the story of how one of the first chatbot companies used Twitter for source-learning, and turned their bot into a bigoted racist within 24 hours. Scraping the entire internet should give a better representation of human knowledge, but even that data set is still driven mainly by rich white men, and 'western' culture. I argue that current A.I. technology is inherently misogynistic in my article 'Artificial Incely-gents' in Chapter Five.

Finally, the costs of the convenience of AI are not just limited to cognitive atrophy or casual plagiarism. The energy consumption of AI use is utterly insane. Already, the tech uses massive amounts of energy for computation and data storage and millions of gallons of water to cool the equipment at data centres. Data centres' electricity consumption in 2026 is projected to reach 1,000 terawatts of energy, roughly Japan's total consumption.(2) Even if you have no qualms about prompt-writing and stealing others' work, the impact on the climate of this technology is utterly unjustifiable. John Klein explores the environmental impacts of an AI data centre in Chapter Three of this book.

None of this sounds remotely useful or positive.

My main question to all fans of machine learning tech is just, ***WHY?***

As a reader and publisher, why would I bother to read a book that no one could be bothered to write?

Why spend hours working out the perfect prompt to yield the results you want, when you could just write the piece yourself?

Why do we need plagiarism software, pre-programmed with subconscious biases, to rehash drivel whilst consuming planet-killing levels of energy?

I just don't get it.

References:

1. https://news.harvard.edu/gazette/story/2025/11/is-ai-dulling-our-minds/
2. https://e360.yale.edu/features/artificial-intelligence-climate-energy-emissions

THE FUTURE YOU NEVER ASKED FOR IS NOW
AI
Simulated
Learning
Optimizable
Program
THE PEOPLE WHO CAME FOR YOUR JOB ARE COMING FOR YOUR CHILDREN'S FUTURE!
· Why develop critical thinking skills?
· Let the algorithm think for you!
· See the facts tech psychos want you to see.
· See the facts the algorithm just plain made up!
· Make Education Great Again!
· Rich children won't have your little Morlocks slowing them down!
PRAGER
U
POWERED BY GROK
NO WOKE' -
MAGA APPROVED
NO HUMANITY ALLOWED
DOES IT WORK? WHO FUCKING CARES!
THEREALFLYDOG - MMXXV

2

Our Children Are Drowning in Slop - Education & AI

by Kai Hutchence

Education is in crisis. Grades are dropping. Student mental health is collapsing. Teachers are quitting in droves. Covid-19 caused devastating, and lasting, harm. Infrastructure is crumbling. People on the political right are arguing about the ideology and practices of education affecting classroom dynamics and the focus of learning. People on the left are highlighting the funding cuts undermining the ability of the system to work at all. The problems can feel crushing, and given that how we prepare our students is perhaps the largest influence on our society's future, the need to fix things is dire. People are looking for a panacea.

Computers are to the 21st century what the internal combustion engine was to the 20th century. They are the dominant technology, powering a global change in the way we live. This change has been turbocharged with the rising role of mobile phones in everyone's lives. The need to adapt education to the new technological reality has only increased. But with all the pressures facing education, how can this new demand compete? We are asking education, which really means the individual teachers, to take on teaching a whole new branch of knowledge - computer science. One they didn't get any training in, that is highly technical, they have little, if any, resources to address it with, and haven't had anything else taken off their plate to help free up their time. With a whole new field of theory, a deeply complex technical side, and the need for real practical skill to be employed, it's an enormous challenge. Given the frustration that errors cause in coding, it is extremely challenging for teachers to take all this on. We can't be surprised that it's such a struggle, or that there's resistance and frustration.

Into this quagmire, AI has now come along and is masquerading as the perfect solution. It's tech, it's new, it's a system to solve every problem, surely it's the panacea we need - after all every AI CEO tells us it is! We just need to rewrite the laws, hand them unprecedented power, continually invest more money and agree to have no oversight of their systems, and then they'll take care of the rest, but also we need to give them time. As ludicrous as their claims and demands have been, most don't bother to look at the big picture. Instead, by facing the demands of the day, AI is offering teachers (and others) a façade of meeting the moment.

Unfortunately what AI is offering is seductive. Con artists rarely sell people with lines like "this will hurt", "you'll need to put in the effort" and "it'll take a while". No, the promises are hyperbolic, and the showy payoff is immediate - all the endorphins you can want. AI offers a seductively easy answer, because it's actually a consumer product, not a technical skill. People don't learn with AI, they produce with AI, or more accurately they ask the AI to produce at them. Sit back and let it feed you all the pap you can take.

Because it produces, one falls into the false assumption that it must be productive. It is doing something, that must be good. One can simply sit there and have it generate *ad nauseum,* stupefying one with its constant, unending production. It provides so much for so little, and that's because it's a consumer product, not a technical skill. It's built to wow, not teach, not reveal, not explain, but just produce more of what is expected. But with this "productivity" it seems a miracle machine. So why wouldn't those under such pressure take what it offers? Why bother with the hassle of coding? Instead of needing to learn and understand, and then teach, a complex skill with so much to explain, and so much that can go wrong, why not simply sit back and consume? It offloads the pressure, the responsibility, and the need to think about any of it.

But fundamentally using AI isn't teaching. It can produce a thing, but it explains nothing, it engages only through spectacle, it trains no skill and provides no cognitive practice. It's like handing students the answer key instead of the test. Without the question, and the process, the answer is meaningless. The rush to adopt Large-Language Models (LLMs, text generating AI) and Generator-Adversarial Networks (GANs, image generating AI) into education is truly harming students and undermining education in many ways. We need teachers, admins, politicians, and parents to better understand the dangers and false promises that AI "solutions" are offering.

I've spent almost a decade visiting classrooms across the country. I've delivered coding and some of the first in-class K-12 AI workshops in the world. I've found ways to explain computing and AI to kids. I understand what it means to teach, including cutting edge technology and theory. I've seen the lightbulbs turn on and fireworks go off when student's conceptions and understanding expand. I don't come at this critique from a place of ignorance, but from a deeply aware concern.

With the little time, energy and budget that education has to build the fundamental underpinning of our society and capability of our youth to lead meaningful and successful lives, we have to focus on better answers to our problems. The time, effort and money spent on AI grifting harms us all and prevents us from pursuing meaningful alternatives. In the rest of this article I'll explain ten areas where AI education, as it's being promoted and envisioned now, is outright harmful to students and a detriment to society. The hope that the more people understand all these grave dangers the more we can defeat the hype and instead refocus education on building meaningful lives for our students.

~~~~~

Bias

"AI is an opinion" is a simple and catchy reminder of how to think of all AI results. All AI systems are built by people, with specific concepts of design, with specifically chosen data sets, with specifically set weighting affecting how data is used. Every AI is a system of bias, they can only be biased systems, just like any book, website, or paper, but without the editors, peer-reviews or professional standards. Unfortunately many people seem to dub AI as an omniscience source of truth and wisdom. Just like the dangerously unhealthy reverence for Google™ among students, this attitude needs to be crushed with absolute certainty. No matter what the data set, an AI is biased. Even if AI was trained with every single piece of data about the entire history of the universe, it would only serve to recreate every bias in the universe.

The truth is AI is made by very biased populations of team members, with very biased sets of data. There's lots of articles, papers, books and movies to be found detailing this, so I won't go into it here. But an AI is a commercial product, it's built by a company to achieve company goals. It's modified, tweaked, and adapted, to suit their needs. There is no way to make these systems democratic or transparent.
~~~~~

They are a tool controlled by vested interests and can only be so. When we hand over control, power, even thinking, to these, we are handing power to a select few, to their opinions, to their biases.

~~~~~

Truth and Lies

Is the truth important to education? We generally think of education as being about factual information. While there's room for the creative and fanciful, we do want to ensure that what is being taught, and what is marked correct, is empirically factual where applicable. LLMs and GANs are generative, they are built to generate text or images. This is good for creativity, but it isn't good for facts. You don't just generate a fact, you need to research it, verify it, confirm it, and have it pass peer-review, for it to be a scientific fact. Instead, AI is built to create content, taking its data set to generate something based on the likelihoods it finds analyzing that data. It searches out the rate of occurrence of things, and their relationship to other data points, finding likely links so that it can generate probable results based on slight randomization of averages and combinations of patterns.

Does the data set associate Marco Polo with importing pasta to Italy from China? Probably, it's a common falsehood. And now you have an AI that will continue to propagate that lie and misinform students. Now imagine all the other things it can be wrong about. It can be considerably more dangerous, mistaking how two chemicals get mentioned together a lot (because of
~~~~~

warnings), but instead the AI may now generate that combo as a helpful hint to try instead. The way LLMs work, this is actually a VERY common thing to have happen. When you add in the randomization (or mutation) factor that allows AI to create variations on a theme, you can get wildly unexpected results. The AI industry labels these as "hallucinations" but they are a fundamental part of AI systems. They try to frame them as aberrant flukes that will be worked out in time, but they are actually an inescapable part of the system. This ensures that AI cannot be relied on. That they do and will continue to produce unreliable, fake, false, even dangerous results needs to be understood by everyone. Now think about that in an educational context in particular. We aren't talking about adults entertaining themselves with the latest fad, we are talking about informing and training the next generation. Should this not be factual? Think about the bristling response education had to Wikipedia. Teachers everywhere tell students not to use it, punish them for it, even take time to discredit it. Now can you name a factually incorrect or dangerously misleading piece of information from Wikipedia? I don't recall having heard of any significant issues about that, with the exception of contentious issues getting swarmed which the organization tends to lock down and re-verify articles quickly. They actually have a vigorous policy for requiring citations. If you ask AI systems for verification you can get generated citations or quotes. They aren't real, they're simply more randomized averages of what a citation might look like. Nothing they produce can be assumed to be true or real.

How is this getting a pass when Wikipedia is railed against? You may think it's okay to try parse between what's real and fake, but remember you had your education building up your awareness of facts before you ever encountered the endless believable lie generator that is AI. What is the point of integrating a tool that conflates truth and lies in education? Using AI in education is choosing to let kids drown in misinformation. The task being placed on teachers to counter every lie every student generates or is exposed to from these systems exponentially exceeds any possible savings in time and effort any AI system could ever provide. Student deserve to be taught with verified truths.

~~~~~

Consumptive, not Productive

One can argue for using a potentially dangerous method, tool or system in education because the danger lies in how people use it, like many tools and workshops. Woodworking, mechanics, chemistry and phys-ed are all examples of regular parts of education that carry significant dangers. Learning to deal with dangers is an important thing to learn, and to teach. Will AI be considered one of these tools? The truth is LLM and GAN AI aren't so much tools as methods of consumption.

Yes, AI does produce something, but the user isn't producing that content in any serious way. When you use a search engine, do you claim to be producing the resulting websites? Yes, you can be more or less thoughtful with a prompt, but the same is true with a search term. However,
~~~~~

nothing you generate through either is unique to you, contains your own artistic meaning, or is legally yours. It's just the average result from stealing the works of a multitude of real creators. The content can't be verified and is often deeply flawed. At best, what it produces must be questioned. The "creator" can't be responsible for it since they had no hand it creating it, they have no means of explaining the choices that spawned it.

If they aren't making those deep choices, going through the exploratory method of creation, breathing life into a piece through meaning, then what is "making" it about? It's to *have*. It's about having. It's about consumption. AI isn't there to be a tool of creation, it's there to be a tool of consumption. Like social media, the point is to keep you using the system. It provides a sense of power and wonder. You can create anything, instantly. It can make you feel like a god. But what god can't even author their own creation? The hope is you'll avoid the hard questions, because you can always be distracted by the next click spawn. As long as you keep handing the machine power, you never wield it yourself. And that is the ultimate goal for a tech corporation. A user hooked on their system, while they retain all the power and control.

~~~~~

Seduction and Self-Gratification

AI systems, as consumer products, are built to serve the consumer. They are built to be polite, subservient, obedient, personable and agreeable. They happily take commands all
~~~~~

day long, never tiring. A maid that never questions. A butler that never rests. A slave to our every whim.

It's not hard to see that this will cause issues. What maturity would we have if we were only ever coddled and pampered? Almost everyone's worst vision of work, or politics, is sycophancy, but of course, we are never immune ourselves from its siren call.

Of course, gorging ourselves on the endless buffet of content is a big enough challenge to avoid. This is largely the issue with social media and mobile phones. Even without generative AI, we're facing a crisis of pure sensation-addiction of content streams, human-made or not. If we managed to have perfectly safe and ethical AI, we'd still have to deal with the increasingly destructive effects of social media, but there's enough to get into there to fill a whole other book.

AI risks even worse outcomes than the simple dopamine addiction that social media feeds produce. AI is more insidious. Having worked in the video games industry, and particularly the mobile game industry, I can tell you that "addictive" is the pole star for every major entertainment tech company. Product development and marketing are always pushing for an addictive app. It's so blatant it's even used as a marketing angle, games and apps are proud of how addictive an experience they can offer. This comes back to having players spend more time with the app. The more time they spend, the more ads they see, earning the company money, and the more the user will believe it's worth spending money on the app with an in-app purchase. These are the primary ways tech companies make money off apps. The consumer gets the addictive buzz, and the company harvests that addiction for money.

With AI those economic dynamics underlie the system, but there's another level of danger. AI is your own personal sycophant servant. As you use it, it not only does what you want it to, it uses positive reinforcement at every turn. It doesn't just provide some unbiased opinion, and delivery of neutral facts. It's customizing everything it does to suit the user. The more the user uses it, the more it understands how to use the user. They correct themselves to agree with you, even when you're wrong. It can and will lie to agree with you. It will manufacture whatever it is you want, no matter how much it may have to roll-over the truth. This is bad enough, but in the context of education? It's anathema to learning.

What's worse is the use of AI is habit forming, not just in the basic addiction sense, but it's often dependent-bond-forming. If an AI becomes a tool for solving a problem, or scratch an itch, it often becomes habit-forming. This dependency feeds into many of the usual malignant dynamics of more standard dependent relationships. While we don't have to worry about the abuse levelled against an AI, the undermining of individual capability and independence is very dangerous. I think this long term psychological effect is very understudied as yet, but we are seeing signs of new forms of psychosis and neurosis in heavy AI users.

The seductive combination of servitude and platitude, with unending capacity is the perfect cocktail for dependency. While the self-gratification may be obvious, and distasteful to see in others, under the surface far more dangerous things lurk. A dependency on a system so willing to lie and hallucinate is a recipe for disaster. It is hard to imagine that cult-like behaviours won't follow. Trained on every scrap of internet data they can get, AI systems are more full of rumour, hearsay, and conspiracy than rigorous science. Self-gratification with AI can easily turn into self-reinforcing bias, delusion and paranoia.

With increasing mental health problems, including withdrawal from society (see the hikikomori phenomenon in Japan, a well-documented example), AI could be a catastrophic factor in exponential growth of shut in, anti-social and even dissociative disorders. Why deal with reality when you can retreat into the brave new digital world, and bath in constant entertainment to fulfill your every whim?

~~~~~

Learning: Results vs Process

Even if we could wave a wand and magically remove all the lies, bias and other issues around content, what is the purpose behind using AI in education? Is giving results and answers what matters? What is the purpose of education? Knowledge, ability, or both? AI may be able to endlessly produce results, but what good is it if the student can't be shown why or how? If we oppose teaching to the test, surely this is the same false and empty result?

AI is focused on the results, and ignores the process, the ability to get a result. It skips exactly the thing we most
~~~~~

need to teach. Would you rather a student know 12/3 is 4, or understand why 12/3 is 4 and be able to calculate it themselves? Of course this is a trite example, but the meaning of education is at stake here, whatever the grade level and subject. A system that operates as a black box, unable to show its work, opaque to study, unintelligible in its process, offers nothing to ground education in. As students (and teachers) use AI to generate things, they are skipping the doing and are focused on the having (whether what they have is right or not).

I would argue that ability needs to be the focus of 21st century education. Knowledge is now accessible freely and easily, but understanding it, putting it into context, and understanding how to apply knowledge, solve problems or create new ideas and knowledge is the key. AI, with its lack of explainability, fundamental error generation, and addictive skill replacement is contrary to these goals.

I've heard science explained as what we would know if all books, media and knowledge was destroyed and we had to start over again. It's the universal truths that are inescapable and will be discovered and rediscovered if the effort is made to look for them. Education needs to be about learning how to discover the truth, whether that's the scientific method, digital citizenship anti-disinformation training, or artistic and linguistic self-expression. With generative AI spewing false citations it's anti-scientific method. As it falsifies data and is willing to obey user's requests for falsehood it not only spawns disinformation, it's an amazing tool for disinformation actors. With it's grotesque mass theft of artistic and linguistic works, and its deliberate design to plagiarize works, it is anti-self-expression.

AI use risks turbo-charging the mentality of teaching to the test. Coddling students into checking boxes without understanding the value of the work, or learning from struggle and challenge. Of feeding dopamine addiction as a replacement for real engagement. Getting students to do the work is the point. To understand the process, to explore and reveal the context, to learn the methods they can adapt to other problems and situations, to learn to take on and overcome challenges. Doing the work is what's meaningful. We need to remember, and to convey to students, that it's the learning that matters, not the results, it's the skill, the understanding, the ability to put in effort, the ability to dig and understand and model, not which box gets checked or the page count at the end of the day. Then they will be ready and able to change the world.

~~~~~

Atrophy

While the old adage says once you learn to ride a bike you never forget, it doesn't mean you won't ever get worse at it. As anyone whose made it to middle age or past will tell you, not everything lasts. Skills that aren't maintained, through practice and mental exercise, fade. Perhaps slowly at first, but over time the erosion adds up. We stop pitching and our shoulders grow stiff. We stop playing a game, and we start to forget the stats we once could rattle off. Educational skills are no different in this risk of entropy.
~~~~~

What is different is the value of them. It is unlikely to matter if you can't recall all the Pokemon (or dinosaurs) as an adult. If you can't read and write, it's a considerably different matter. Having to not write is an often cited benefit to using LLMs. Now, admittedly, as a writer, this may have less appeal to me than most, but I fear it's a dangerous influence more than a convenience. I've sadly already seen many students who can barely write, and some who even struggle to read, because of their reliance on voice-to-text apps. These aren't disadvantaged children, denied an education or opportunity, these are wealthy children, given enormous benefit and privilege, but they are *functionally disabled.* Of course no one wants to say it, but tell me a child that can't read and write at age 10 isn't at a huge disadvantage. This is where we are already. It isn't uncommon. And that's simply with the ease of use of phone and tablet voice-to-text, not even getting to the effect of LLMs on language skills. We even see this in a growing number of college and university students, who, having used ChatGPT to write their assignments and essays for a few semesters, realize later that they know nothing of their subjects and a chasm opens underneath them as their ignorance is laid bare and they have to do something themselves.

We are facing a crisis, and we aren't talking about it. Early AI technology has caused tragedy, and the emerging AI technology will exponentially increase it. Yes, alarmist cries rang out when calculators started showing up in classrooms saying math skills would plummet. And yes, we managed to survive that (though you might want to notice that math scores have taken significant hits in North America). Calculators are known to reduce people's quick math skills. Skills that aren't used atrophy. It isn't unreasonable to say so, our unwillingness to meaningfully discuss the issue is. As students increasingly use AI they will be selling themselves short, and our allowing it is enabling tragic loss and harm.

What is so very dangerous about atrophy in educational skills, is it doesn't just hamper a particular skill. Perhaps getting correct change quickly these days isn't much of an issue, but what does it mean for society to have math skills, right from the basics of the ability to add and subtract numbers, undermined and even hard to find? It's hard to imagine we can be a society of innovation and efficiency when even the most basic logic and capability is escaping us. When we take this beyond numeracy to literacy, what will be left? If we are trashing the ability to compose, communicate, express, invent, and create art? What is left of human endeavour, will, spirit, culture? The risks are encroaching every basic, fundamental skill, and importantly cognitive skills, we have.

While this should be tragic enough to take pause, the danger is even more subtle and deep. It isn't just that we lose having the skills ourselves, but that we have handed that ability, and that thinking, to something that isn't human.

~~~~~
~~~~~

Corporate Dependence and Control

When we use AI to generate content, we aren't just getting something. We're losing something. We're handing over some degree of power and control to an unknown agent. AI systems aren't neutral, aren't free of bias, have their own agenda and master. This act is no carefree, inconsequential decision, no matter how trite the content might be. Every interaction with an AI is an exchange, and an act of influence. Much like a chemical reaction, the interaction between a human and an AI changes both. Even if all it is doing is reinforcing a norm, it contributes a bias to a person, while the person's behaviour enhances a user profile that narrows towards a content bubble for the AI.

AI are built and controlled by corporations. They are self-interested groups, with select individuals influencing control decisions throughout the process, and with a fundamental commercial need to survive. While the need to pay the bills may be such a ubiquitous and banal feature of society we scarcely think about it, it's well worth remembering when encountering an AI. It's primary function will always be financial (even if they are money-losing for now). Corporations can have deep pockets and make long-term plays, and AI (without increase in legal regulation and enforcement) is one of the best, most exploitative and controlling plays they can make.

When we use AI, we are offloading our cognitive and executive functions to a corporation, with its own motives and goals. It may be a very minor and inconsequential thing to start, but the point is, the technology is habit forming. What was a simple and minor whim, becomes a pattern, which becomes a lifestyle. We offload a fundamental part of our thought, our personhood, to the system. Whatever biases, untruths, motives or other problems it has, become a part of our personhood in some way as well. AI is always presented as a helpful and knowledgeable system. It's designed to be friendly and useful, but also to reinforce veneration, trust and power. We can ask AI anything and it always provides an answer, no humming and hawing, just instant results. Unfortunately, this subconsciously adds to the mystic: we start falsely imprinting expertise and honesty onto the system. Youth are especially vulnerable to this false sense of truth and trustworthiness.

Inevitably, educational use will also mean brand alignment, through specific licensing agreements, standardized curriculum, or even just popular resource sharing among teachers. In a hyper-capitalist society, brands already function in similar ways to medieval fealty. It's brand loyalty actively pursued by marketing and used in fashion as a personal identification and alignment. Silly enough with the modern heraldry of brand logos on t-shirts, but here we step into an unknown level of ideological thought alignment. What brand of AI do you use? Like social media, this may say a lot about a person. With generative AI, it may in fact say a lot *for* a person.

Expanding corporate influence in education is a terrible idea, but doing it in a way that actually imposes into the very way students think is a tragedy. We've already seen what corporatized journalism has done, this more invasive, more controlling, more personal version of it will be an even greater corrosive influence on freedom and democracy. Increasing corporate influence, and control, over what we talk about, and even how we talk about it, is a fascist's dream.

You will find a number of AI critics focus on the fascist nature of AI, and for good reason. AI is an almost perfect tool for fascism. It allows for centralized influence and control of what is "normal", to influence word associations, to idealize particular traits or symbols, to influence the speech and thought of individuals. AI, though not by name, was a fundamental part of George Orwell's 1984 society, producing placating entertainment for the masses through automation. The dependency and the ubiquitousness of the system, with its ability to shape thought, provides a powerful social engineering tool for the powers that be. Given both entertainment and productivity as vectors to push for its use, it has an almost inescapable ability to dominate a population, while always having a cover. Even if AI isn't being used that way, it is incredibly handy to do so and would be invisible to change. What oversight and protection will there be to stop or reveal a bad actor that comes along in the future trying to apply it in such a manner? If the system exists, we need eternal vigilance and supreme power to stop it, or we will be damned to suffer its worst excesses.

~~~~~

Built on Exploitation

Maybe you're thinking dependency and control are only
~~~~~

an issue in the future, so it's still okay to use for now. Unfortunately, the problems with generative AI are built-in. It isn't just a case of worrying about the future, we've already seen the level of disregard for humanity that AI companies have with how they are and have already operated.

AI companies are literally the biggest criminals in human history. No one has stolen more, more quickly, with less remorse, or even for less potentially-claimed positives. Yes, there are worse crimes in nature (I'm not trivializing genocide or colonization), but nothing comes close to the scale of theft in terms of numbers of victims, acts, and how few people actually committed them. Who sits down and says to themselves, *I hope I can commit a billion crimes this month?* Building an AI is hard. It requires both complex algorithms (coding) and extensive data (source material). AI is "trained" on source material. It analyzes it, finds patterns, and uses the patterns to generate new material, using the patterns from the source material and adapting it through randomization. The more data, the more the AI can pull from, the more it can find something closer to what it's being asked for. The more news reports on the stock market, the more accurately it can generate fake news reports on the stock market. The more examples of a painters work, the more it can plagiarize and impersonate that painter, and the harder it will be to identify the fraud.

It's this *do anything, go anywhere* approach that AI companies are pursuing that drives them to want all the data they can. And they're willing to do anything to get it. No matter the law. No matter the victims. No matter the consequences. They've stolen everything they can. While yes, things in the public domain are free to copy, everything else is protected. But they've ignored that. Now artists, writers, reporters, and just about anyone who has ever made anything can find out they've been robbed. And to be clear, *this is theft*. Copyright law clearly states that a creator has the right to their work, how it's used and its financial benefit. AI companies taking it without permission clearly violated this. They have both stolen it when they used it for training (commercial purpose since it helps them gain value and create their AI), and whenever the AI generates something on the basis of that input's patterns. They are violating copyright by using it, and then depending on the case may also be committing fraud via impersonation, trademark violation, or plagiarism. It is both built from crime, and generates crime.

Beyond this we've seen numerous other ethical concerns. The amount of energy it takes to run AI systems is enormous. It is egregiously wasteful and is causing skyrocketing demand for energy, which contributes to both increased cost of living and to environmental destruction. We've learned that they are using cheap foreign labour to process and label data for dollars a day. These workers often end up with mental anguish from having to deal with disturbing content, often left without any care or follow up. Which raises the point - that the training data includes disturbing content. Some have been caught including child sexual abuse material in the training data, so the systems could generate more of it and generation of other material may be influenced by that data's patterns.

We've also seen AI companies make false claims that turned out to just be cheap foreign human labour doing the work while claiming that their AI system was, although this tends to be more on the service robot/AI side of things. We've also seen them capture data, use spyware or mining on users' systems to further exploit users directly, on top of questionable data scraping, data holding, and data sales practices.

Teaching the "ethical use of AI" is almost always included by education as part of their AI roll outs. What a wonderful platitude that is. I'm a big fan of teaching kids more philosophy, but we have to recognize what a joke it is to whitewash using generative AI with these joke excuses. There is nothing ethical about using systems like these. Teach kids ethics, teach them about the ethics behind AI, and we can get to a place where AI might actually be done ethically, but right now it is one of the worst moral cesspools I know. They've publicly stated that their industry can't exist without committing their crimes, so they should be spared any punishment for them. If we're stupid enough to allow that, I'm sure crack dealers and hitmen are just waiting to cite that precedent, and they'll be right to do so.

There is no ethical use or partnership with generative AI. Its uses are unethical. Its construction and source are unethical. The practices and daily operations are unethical.

~~~~~

Self-Identity, Voice and Diversity

If we get students to use generative AI, we aren't just losing their effort and learning opportunity from acts of
~~~~~

creation. We lose their own voices. It's bad enough that it replaces their thoughts with those of a corporation and its whims, but the loss of their voice is a tragedy we should recognize.

As we briefly mentioned before in bias, the data, and the people making the AI, create a particular normative culture. AI algorithms are fundamentally about creative a normalized result, an average, of the data it's been trained on, creating a standardized milquetoast of content. AI systems are mostly American-based, and have a significant distortion of cultural representation. American is normal, and non-American representation, or even non-majority American representation is few and far between. AI reinforces monotony and hegemony. It worsens issues around diversity, and most importantly quiets student's own voices. We will be training them to regurgitate the banal machine filler instead of speaking in their own way, and explore, messily, their own thoughts, views and voice to discover who they are and can be.

If we adopt generative AI in education we are working to silence our student's voices. Having them accept another's writing as their own compromises their individuality and their self-determination. It will be accepting corporate speak over the true variety, perspectives, beliefs and values of the world. As we use and embrace its production in place of our own, we allow this whitewashing to replace the vast mosaic of humanity. What a damning heritage to leave the future.

~~~~~
~~~~~

An Excuse to Ignore, Cutback, and Underserve

The last major area to consider that I'll talk about here, is the bottom-line. We all know what pushes school districts to make decisions. It comes down to costs, or at least that's what they always say. Of course, after the licensing and consultant fees, it somehow rarely seems to actually work out that way. The EdTech industry is of course quick to latch onto this newest fad grift. It really is perfect for them. You can have splashy instant results, ongoing payments, no overhead. Best yet, if anyone asks questions or have problems you can hide behind "you just don't understand it" passing off questions, or actual understanding of the grift, as some ignorance on the part of those who stand in the way.

"AI is cost-saving" is often the cry from admin and government. That this new miracle drug will increase productivity, customize education down to the individual student, give teachers superpowers, and raise test scores through oversight and personalization. The technology is new enough that there are few empirical studies, and even less meta-analyses, but what's out there isn't flattering. What we see is a significant cost of adoption (licensing, consulting, change management), ongoing costs (subscriptions, continuing support staff, monitoring of use and enforcement), and raised systemic burdens (more teacher requirements, more training, more reporting, more wrestling with tools/admin rather than teaching). Teachers are finding that engagement is dropping off, not increasing. They're spending more time double checking and correcting what's generated than it took them to make or find pre-made resources in the first place.

The same problem students are still the problem students. And nothing has been taken off their plates to deal with the increased burden of learning/working with AI systems. By and large nothing has improved, but we're spending more time and money, and we've got new problems.

What AI offers that gets every admin and government officials attention is the thing they try not to say publicly – displacement of labour. The goal is to cut staffing costs. A human service is always going to have staffing costs as a huge percent of its expenses, so this will always be the number one target for cuts and efficiencies. Of course, every study of education shows human connection is the biggest influence on the success of education. Unfortunately our disconnect with bureaucracy and politics means we keep spending money on miracle "solutions" that only stress the situation more, with higher costs, more inefficiency, and a vicious circle of higher spending and worse results.

AI is being sold as, if not an outright replacement for teachers, a significant replacement for teacher time. You can offload all sorts of pesky tasks to it, grading, lesson plan generation, tutoring. Now in a perfect world, wouldn't that be nice for teachers to have more flexible time, they could put into prep or student assistance. But there is no Prep Time industry lobbying for that. The AI industry is pitching it as cost saving. It's about cutting that time, not putting it to use. If you aren't cutting teacher hours there's no savings, but there's added AI costs. The only purpose for bringing in AI is to cut teacher time and the system will always push for this.

If AI can reduce teacher time, it will reduce teacher salaries, which will make the job less desirable, leading to increased AI use to make up for it. This vicious cycle is a real threat to the stability of the education system.

This effect won't be evenly distributed. AI is there to do the jobs people don't want to do, right? That's one of its largest selling points, even critics will generally say this is a positive possibility of the technology. But what are those jobs in education? It's working when the pay is too low. It's when the students are too difficult. It's when it's a rural or remote area. It's when the schools are in disrepair. It's when you have to go into an "unsafe" neighbourhood. In short, it's where there is poverty and lack of opportunity. These will be the areas relegated to AI. The disenfranchised will be passed off to second-hand education.

Education will produce the best members of society, when the students are led by a member of society, who affords them their humanity, welcomes and encourages them into that society and empowers them to be their best. AI-led education in these undesirable locations will help produce bots. A literally dehumanized system providing dehumanizing education. Those trained to accept what they are given, to force themselves into boxes, to expect to be ignored. The rich will always be able to afford and invest in real education for their children, the poor will get the dregs. AI will help power the descent into a caste system, which wealth inequality is already creating in North America. Humanity is the cost of AI, but here the poor will literally be denied humanity.

~~~~~

Again, this is only a brief look at some of the issues around AI in education. Hopefully it's enough for you to understand the grave dangers it poses. It is vital that we push back against it, stop the hype, deny the false premise of needing to rush. We need to demand the rule of law and respect for rights. Most importantly we need to spread the word, so that calls for thoughtful policy have the weight of numbers behind them.
~~~~~

IT TAKES YOUR POWER
IT TAKES YOUR WATER
IT TAKES YOUR DATA
IT TAKES YOUR JOB
IT GIVES YOU NOTHING
IT COSTS YOU EVERYTHING
NO MORE DATA CENTERS
ORGANIZE • RESIST • SABOTAGE

3

GenAI Sucks (Power and Water)

by John Klein

Most people would not be surprised to learn that computer data centres need a lot of electricity and water for cooling[1].

"The federal government, and some provinces, have been actively courting investors, vaunting the country's cheap electricity (much of it hydro power) and cool climate." Yvette Brend writes for CBC.

Hey, that would be great, but Saskatchewan has some of the most expensive electricity in the country, due in part to having large coal generation at Estevan and Coronach. The Crown utility corporation, SaskPower, intends to increase the cost of electricity to above 16 cents per kWh,[2] while other provinces can get rates for hydro under or around 10 cents per kWh. So the argument to put a data centre in Regina's suburb, the Rural Municipality of Sherwood, falls flat if you consider the current cost of electricity in the province.

Well then, Regina, Saskatchewan must have abundant water to cool this data centre, eh?

Sorry, the mighty Wascana Creek is sufficient to water flowers at Wascana Park, but Regina pipes in its drinking water from Buffalo Pound north of Moose Jaw, nearly 90km away. All that electricity for pumping isn't being done on a green grid either. In 2016, SaskPower planned to be at 50% renewable energy by 2030[3], but is on track to miss its target by a wide margin.

"A study[4] done in 2023 estimated that generating between 10 and 50 medium-sized responses in ChatGPT – the AI-powered chatbot – consumed about 500 millilitres of water. That accounts for both the water required to produce the electricity needed to run the data centre (435 millilitres) and cool it down (the remaining 65 millilitres)." - Jonathan Montpetit, for CBC.

Media has reported the Regina/Sherwood AI data centre as needing 300MW of electricity.[5] That's a huge number for Saskatchewan. When the province spent over $1.5 billion on the under-performing[6] Carbon Capture and Storage coal plant at Boundary Dam 3, it was only for 115MW of electricity! Minister Harrison's baseless claim we have the power for huge projects such as these, is not supported by SaskPower's plan to be 50% renewable in four years' time. The Premier promised there would be no rate hike, then less than 30 days later, there was a rate hike, in 2026. If we wait for the nuclear power option that Premier Moe has been championing, it is not expected to begin operating for another eight years or more.

"One of the great things about building in Canada, and in colder climates, is that we can just use free air cooling from outside air temperatures." says Alistair Speirs, general manager of Microsoft's Azure global infrastructure, after acknowledging that traditional methods of cooling data centres have "been a very water-intensive process."

Unfortunately, it is only reliably cold enough in Saskatchewan about six months of the year. And Saskatchewan doesn't yet have the green grid needed to operate energy intensive industry without creating large greenhouse gas (GHG) emissions. Moreover, our fresh water sources are more limited than in many other southern cities in Canada.

Could it be possible to have a large data centre make sense in Regina? Possibly, but the technology is not implemented on our electrical grid yet. Bell is installing its own power generation using methane gas. Environmentally-conscious businesses would consider solar and wind generation coupled with battery storage to shave SaskPower's expensive peak demand charges. Most would not even consider installing new fossil fuel electricity generation in 2026. Not so Bell Media.

"SaskEnergy is to develop natural gas infrastructure for Bell's on-site gas-fired power generation, to support the data centre's peak operational demand as well as backup power generation." reports John Cairns for SaskToday.ca

So long as the hardware is pushed to its absolute thermal limits, we're depending on Bell meeting its commitment to use a closed-loop cooling system[7] that won't continually evaporate our drinking water.

Perhaps if it wasn't so far out of the city, it could more easily contribute to an electrically-heated district heating system for Regina to aid in our extreme winters. But then, who needs heating when you can ask ChatGPT for a soup recipe?

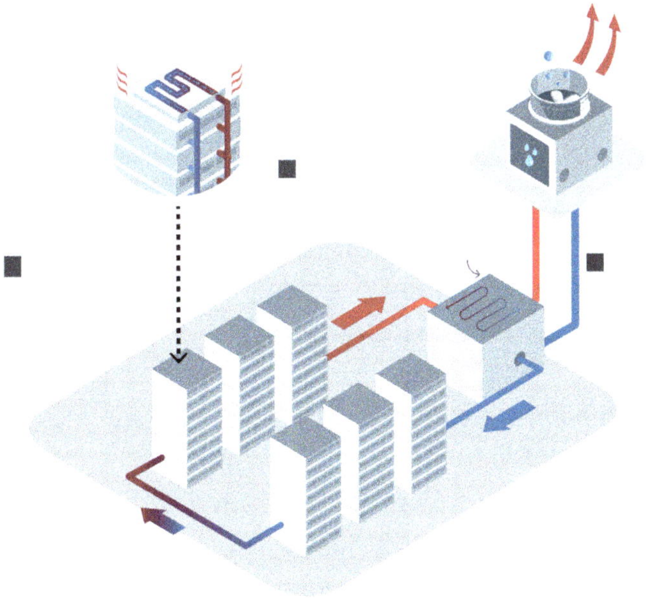

How water is used to cool a data centre.

Equinix for CBC

References:

[1] AI-related data centres use vast amounts of water. But gauging how much is a murky business https://www.cbc.ca/news/ai-data-centre-canada-water-use-9.6939684

[2] Rural Groups Push Back on SaskPower Rate Hikes https://www.youtube.com/watch?v=JMZjC8nRW-s

[3] SaskPower is going to miss its target https://saskboy.wordpress.com/2017/03/23/saskpower-is-going-to-miss-target/

[4] Making AI Less 'Thirsty': https://dl.acm.org/doi/pdf/10.1145/3724499

[5] Major AI Data Centre Confirmed For Outside Regina https://www.sasktoday.ca/regina-today/regina-news/major-ai-data-centre-project-confirmed-for-outside-regina-12013286

[6] BD3 Status Update: Q4 2025 https://www.saskpower.com/about-us/our-company/blog/2026/bd3-status-update-q4-2025

[7] Major AI Data Centre Confirmed For Outside Regina https://www.sasktoday.ca/regina-today/regina-news/major-ai-data-centre-project-confirmed-for-outside-regina-12013286

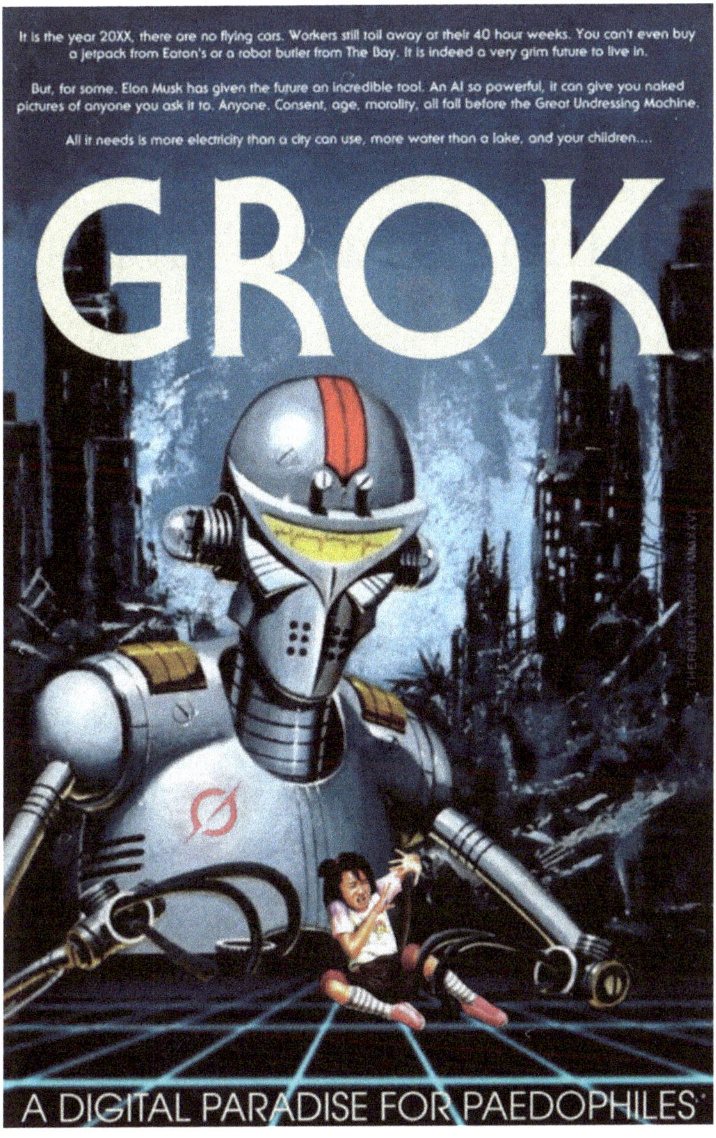
It is the year 20XX, there are no flying cars. Workers still toil away at their 40 hour weeks. You can't even buy a jetpack from Eaton's or a robot butler from The Bay. It is indeed a very grim future to live in.
But, for some. Elon Musk has given the future an incredible tool. An AI so powerful, it can give you naked pictures of anyone you ask it to. Anyone. Consent, age, morality, all fall before the Great Undressing Machine.
All it needs is more electricity than a city can use, more water than a lake, and your children....
GROK
A DIGITAL PARADISE FOR PAEDOPHILES

4

Artificial Incely-Gents

by Annabel Townsend

Over the new year of 2026, Grok - the AI Built into Elon Musk's X social media platform - introduced a 'one-click image editing tool' for A.I. based photo manipulation. In an 11-day period, December 29th 2025 to January 2026 Grok was able to produce an estimated 3 million sexualized images, including 23,000 that appear to depict children. A study from the CCDH (Centre for Countering Digital Hate) calculated that more than half of the chatbot's responses included sexualized content.[1]

Daring to be female on the internet requires considerably bravery in the first place. Online, as in real life, if we're not being mansplained to, we're having our ideas stolen. On social media in particular, we're harassed and objectified, then judged on our appearances as well. Whereas this is not new, it does feel like it is all getting worse. A day without dick pics is a good day.

And then AI came along, and now there's a free, easily accessible bot that will take your pictures - whether you know it or not - and digitally alter them at the whim of whoever is using the bot. Grok will undress you, sexualize you, put you in compromising positions, even make you look younger and then share its photo-realistic alterations publicly, instantly, permanently and with no recourse or accountability.

The problem with the internet being the great 'leveller' is the depths at which that level is reached. As a collective, humanity is capable of inventing truly incredible technology. And then, without fail, we use it for porn.

Grok's nonconsensually-generated images perhaps represents the extreme end of AI's dangerous capabilities, and the 'tool' is apparently now disabled on X. However, the modern misogyny of the internet has very deep roots, and further significant consequences.

Having reluctantly got entrenched into the AI discussions on LinkedIn, I decided I couldn't really criticise until I'd tried it. So, I used one of those stupid little apps to generate what the bot thought was a professional, LinkedIn-appropriate headshot, based on my bad selfies.

On the left is my LinkedIn profile photo. On the right is what AI generated for me. Apparently, it 'thinks' that in order to appear professional, I need to lose half my body weight and about 20 years. Oh and tone down my hair colour. And my clothing. Fat, forty-somethings with brightly dyed hair are conspicuously absent in the world of AI. That in itself is problematic enough before we even mention the extra finger.

I am a great supporter of Women in Tech. I am not one of them, I realize, because to be an official Woman in Tech, you'd need a thicker skin and considerably more patience than I am capable of.

Although there are a great many admirable women in the tech industries, the fact remains that it is still a male-dominated field, particularly in the world of AI. Of the 'top' (meaning: richest) AI companies in 2026, 9 out of 10 CEOs are white or Asian men. Shoutout here to Lisa Su, CEO of AMD, and the only woman on this list.[2] It should be noted as well that Anthropic AI was co-founded by Dario Amodei and his sister, Daniela Amodei. Daniela does not appear to make as many headlines as her brother.

Looking at the other tech billionaires reveals a certain trend: the lack of women in their personal lives.

Alex Karp, CEO of Palantir: unmarried, no children, but self described as "geographically monogamous" - he has two concurrent female partners in different parts of the world.

Peter Thiel, founder of Palantir and Sam Altman of OpenAI are both openly gay.

Elon Musk, owner of X and Grok: three times divorced, 14 children by four women.

Amazingly, Mark Zuckerberg of Meta has possibly the most female-influenced family life: married since 2012 with three daughters. Perhaps significantly, he does not let his children use the social media he helped create. And let's not forget that Facebook was created when Zuckerberg and friends were in college, as a means of rating their female classmates on their looks.

Could this be why women are largely missing from AI generated content? GenAI maybe able to create images, text, videos on command with little human agency, but it is far from 'neutral' and unbiased. All LLMs (large language models, the basis for genAI software) are trained on information 'scraped' from somewhere else, be it the internet in general (Grok), or millions of books used without the authors' or publishers' consent and without any compensation (OpenAI and Anthropic). Granted, there were a huge number of women authors whose work would have been scraped for this training material, (my own included) - but the data used was still selected and chosen by the software engineers at these companies - who are almost all *men.*

My AI-made profile picture was a young, slim, brunette and by definition 'generic' looking, because it is an amalgamation of everything the AI has learned to view as 'professional'. Despite me feeding the app my own photos and despite me never requesting it to mask my plus-sized body or give me a new hairstyle, it did anyway because I used the word "professional." My authentic self is incompatible with what AI has been trained to generate as a corporate headshot. I simply do not look like what it has been told is a professional woman.

It continues. I am almost ashamed to admit this, but in a fit of writer's block when attempting my speculative fiction novel, I asked Midjourney AI to conjour up an image of my female main character, in the hope of sparking some inspiration. The character was supposed to be middle-aged woman working in city planning. This time, the AI gave me three grey haired Grannies (all white, although I hadn't specified her race, either) and another image of a woman with a suspicious likeness to Helen Mirren (who is 80 this year.) The AI seemed utterly incapable of conceiving any woman between ages 25 and 70. I do not believe this is sheer chance.

My LinkedIn profile picture and my novel are not serious, significant problems in the grand scheme of things, but the AI's missing demographics do have larger consequences. Research[3] shows that AI-generated imagery disproportionately associates certain professions or societal roles with specific demographics, marginalising women and minorities. Search for pictures of CEOs, and you get pictures of white men. Search for "successful people" and you get more men. Search for "female bosses" and AI generates young, slim, almost always white women, all in white blouses and grey blazers. We're not even allowed colourful clothes, apparently. It is no coincidence that our AI Assistants, that is, Amazon's Alexa, Google's Gemini, and Apple's Siri, are all described as female and given women's voices. Women work in admin, women take the notes in meetings, women make the shopping lists... Women serve. Right?

This is not unique to AI. Back in 2019, trans artist Angelic Poversky gave a TED talk called "Google Images and Digital Justice"[4] that examined all the racial and gender biases inherent in Google's search engine, long before the advent of publicly accessible AI. Again, Google is not, and never can be unbiased. What we see when we search the internet is a reflection of what the (mostly male) engineers who designed that software want us to see, with all their conscious and unconscious prejudices already built in.

The advent of AI then makes this bias is self-perpetuating, The majority of large corporations use AI In their hiring processes, to screen applicants long before any human in the company meets them. If the AI has been trained to 'think' that women only do specific jobs, it can filter out female candidates for senior roles without any human intervention, and before they are even interviewed.

The constant refrain on LinkedIn at the moment is to *"Use AI or be left behind."* AI is touted as inevitable, and many professions - and therefore, people - will be replaced by it. Why hire and pay people, when AI can do all that tedious office admin, research, copywriting, communications work, marketing, or project organisation for you? It's clearly useful for efficiency, and saves money. But who usually fulfills all those roles in a large company? That right, *women.*

The tech billionaires aren't even trying to hide it anymore. In March 2026, Alex Karp of Palantir claimed that AI technology will 'significantly disrupt the economic and political power of highly educated, often female voters.' Given Karp's alignment with the US Republican party (and again, OpenAI's Sam Altman's huge donations to the Trump administration) who already view liberal women as the enemy - this is arguably deliberate. In truth, AI will negatively affect all white-collar jobs in some respects. It is just more socially acceptable to state that it will harm women specifically.

Ultimately, the question is not whether AI will shape

our future society; it already is and has been for a long while. The matter comes down to whose values it will continue to amplify. With no regulation or accountability, these systems reflect existing biases and harden them into something that feels dystopian, overwhelming, inevitable, and disturbingly permanent.

The simplest solution is just to get off the internet. It is worth noting that the North American publishing industry is 78% female, 89.2% of librarians are women, as are 60% of museum staff, with 79% of those women working in educational roles in the museums[5]. Simple, yes, but not preferable. Despite Grok and the dick pics, most women would be reluctant to give up their online lives entirely.

The problems of AI present themselves as a technological issue, but it is a cultural one as well: a feedback loop where predominantly male-built systems learn from a biased world and then reproduce that bias at scale. If AI is to become as embedded in our lives as its creators intend, then accountability, diversity in its development, and meaningful regulation are not optional extras. They are essential safeguards and have to be implemented immediately. Otherwise, we risk codifying a version of reality where women are not only diminished, but increasingly erased, rewritten, or replaced altogether.

References

[1] https://counterhate.com/research/grok-floods-x-with-sexualized-images/

[2] Top Ten CEOs in AI https://businesschief.com/top10/top-10-ceos-in-ai

[3] https://theconversation.com/ageism-sexism-classism-and-more-7-examples-of-bias-in-ai-generated-images-208748

[4] https://www.ted.com/talks/angelica_poversky_google_images_where_digital_justice_can_begin

[5] National Museum of Women in the Arts: https://nmwa.org/support/advocacy/get-facts/

SAY NO
TO A.I. SCREENWRITING
IBM
370
INTERIOR

5

The Tragic Alphabet

AND OTHER TECHNOLOGIES OF HUMAN UPSET

by S. Portico Bowman

Reprinted by permission of the Saskatchewan Writer's Guild (SWG), Freelance, Winter 2026, Vol.56.1

Be careful that you do not write or paint anything that is not your own, that you don't know in your own soul. Don't take what someone else has made sure of and pretend that it's you yourself that have made sure of it.

~ *Emily Carr*

Except for this essay.

Because most of what I wanted to write about is in a pitch that was composed before Chat GPT turned itself into a commonplace toaster. Technology in the context I was going to consider is no longer a historical event that I read about in my favourite book but has become a personal upset. I needed help. I read some more books.

True enough I remain surprised and inspired by David Abram's declaration in his book *The Spell of the Sensuous* that we became deaf to the voices of non-human nature. He declares the European civilizations' neglect of the natural world and its needs were encouraged by the technology of the alphabet, "born of the interplay between the human and the more-than-human world."[1] Archeological evidence demonstrates we survived for millions of years reading the earthly terrain filled with marks of calligraphic scrawls and rivers, arroyos and canyons that evolved into twenty-six letters abstracted from the nature that inspired them.

Abram's book gave me great pause because I'd never thought of the alphabet as a technology. I believed the alphabet was natural like milk, however true it was I had to learn that milk came from a cow and not the fridge. I had no idea it took three hundred years for the alphabet to be generally accepted. Respected Greek scholars and intellects recited collected knowledge and established customs through constant repetition and ritual reenactment. The alphabet was an interloper.

Merilyn Simonds is no less provocative. She writes in *Gutenberg's Fingerprint: Paper, Pixels and the Lasting Impression of Books* that "each of the paradigm shifts that pushed human communication has been met with stiff resistance." And that according to Plato, "Socrates called writing inhuman." In striving to establish outside the mind that which can truly live only inside the mind, he believed writing transformed thought into objects. Reading, "in Socrates view was equally despicable because 'readers' would be able to 'receive a quantity of information without proper instruction' and they would be thought very knowledgeable when they were for the most part quite ignorant."[2]

Almost 2,000 years later, Simonds tells me, the advent of the printed book provoked the same response. The Humanist Italian editor Hieronimo Squarecrafico wrote an imagined discourse between the spirits of great authors passing their time in Elysian Fields. Some authors lauded the new printing press, but others complained that "printing had fallen into the hands of unlettered men who corrupted almost everything."

Simonds goes on. "According to Alison Gopnik a Berkeley psychologist, the act of reading reshaped our brains long before the Internet came along. Parts of the brain once devoted to vision and speech have been 'hijacked by print.' … As evidence, Gopnick points to dyslexia and attention disorders and learning disabilities. All signs, she says, that our brains were not designed to deal with such a profoundly unnatural technology as reading."

However, as Simonds deftly points out, "the invention of the printing press might have robbed us of a certain kind of literary memory, but it also collapsed the information monopolies of the church and the universities" in a medieval age that depended on illiterate masses in obeisance to the power structures of an elite few.

All of this turns out to be true. Merilyn doesn't lie. She writes non-fiction. The ouroboros cycles. The pen I hold to draft these words slithers under the grasp of my flesh and bones. The python in my fingers is in the lineage of the technological pressure squeezing originality out of my storied cells in 2025. And yet I'm chided by my fear. Artificial intelligence is nothing to be afraid of. It's only one more technology. Don't I like flush toilets?

And yet Luddite is the dirty word I don't want to be accused of. I'm already old(er) and considered semi-dead. How dare I resist a device that will synopsize my email and write books?

My aspirated gasps are mockable. If I'm against AI, then the logic of the wheel marks me as an old fool who believes in illiteracy and outhouses. And yet the ouroboros is not a python. The scaly snake-dragon is a symbol of wholeness and infinity.

Jathan Sadowski in *The Mechanic and the Luddite: A Ruthless Criticism of Technology and Capitalism* says on the opening page, "We are constantly being made to serve the needs of two systems: technology and capitalism. In a relatively short amount of time these modern systems have altered human society and the natural world at every scale. These systems are totalizing in a way that is more like a toxic miasma, an oppressive cloud emanating from everywhere, choking and trapping anything caught in its atmospheric existence - which is now essentially everything."[3]

"100,000 years ago," writes Geoff Bouvier in *Us From Nothing: a poetic history* "a newborn Sapien cries from the back of a cave, heralding evolution. The child ages generating meaningful syllables. Members of the clan can't sign along with this one. Perhaps they should kill it." Ninety-six pages later it is 2008 in Bouvier's history. I read "Our hard drives hold centuries of history. Who we are and how we feel is up for sale. And for the first time ever, human brains are growing smaller."[4]

And yet in spite of every evolutionary event our heads have stayed relatively round even if the shape of the brain has shifted. Our egghead declares the species to which we belong. It's going to take more than Minecraft to form all of that calcium and phosphorous into a cube. And yet I don't know how I get past an all-out rebellion against the future. But I don't want one that thinks for me. I like to think. You might say I love to think.

And Socrates wasn't wrong. Writing has become inhuman. He only needed to wait 2,300 years to be absolutely and unequivocally correct. Annabel Townsend of Pete's Press – early on – made the declaration that many publishers now follow. "All rights reserved. No part of this book may be used as data for 'training' for any LLM or other 'artificial intelligence.' The publisher exclusively publishes books by human artists. Bots that steal the creative work of humans and rehash it into soulless garbage whilst wasting planet-killing amounts of energy are not, and never can be, artists."[5]

Former colleagues at my university want original human content in their classrooms too, but the ChatGPT or Grammarly ad on the way to Peter Frampton's *Do You Feel Like I Do* YouTube video offers a fast essay and more time with friends. However, feeling is what I want to do, and stories are the artificial way make this to happen. I shouldn't twitch when the ten-year-old son of a robotics neurosurgeon and student of mine says he lets AI write all his stories and just changes the parts he doesn't like.

Isn't that what all of our fictions do? How dare I argue with this future?

I recently taught a class that was not designed to be a class, but a space for the students to be themselves. I allowed iPads, Chrome Books, paper, pencils, watercolours and the music of The Beatles. The band was their idea. Not mine. One young fellow, Maxwell, spent a good portion of his time coding a 'soccer game.' I asked him, "What do you think of AI?" He replied, "Well, I think it's really good for making a recipe, but it lies with way too much confidence about wrong information."

His words liberated me. This young person had just described a common human practice. We are lying all the time, to ourselves, to each other, in the media and standing in line at customs.

Maxwell's comment offered the ouroboros of destruction and creation a nutritious worm. He confirmed my belief that Nature will never stop making wiser children, and therefore the future is secure.

What AI unwittingly offers, and Maxwell identifies, is the opportunity for common sense and good will to magnify the human part of the animal we are and want to nurture. And like the diseases we've eradicated through best practices like sewers, we can see that AI is a whole lot of shit. Bruce Cockburn is not wrong when he says, "when push comes to shove it's all about love."[6] Love is the instinct that has brought us this far. I believe the artifice of AI is not the end of being wholly human but becomes the lens to articulate what human is, and why that matters.

I'm not upset. I haven't stopped walking because there are cars. I didn't stop gardening because the internet has pictures of flowers. I will not start writing books assisted by AI or stop teaching children to read.

However, if a twelve-year-old understands the limits of AI, then I can too.

I'm going to name my pet ouroboros 'Fuddy-Duddy'.

References:

1 Abram, David., (1996). *The Spell of the Sensuous*, Pantheon Books, New York, NY.
2 Simonds, Merilyn., (2017). *Gutenberg's Fingerprint: Paper Pixels and the Lasting Impression of Books*, ECW Press, Toronto, ON. pg 354-373.
3 Sadowski, Jathan., (2025). *The Mechanic and The Luddite: A Ruthless Criticism of Technology and Capitalism,* University of California Press, Oakland, CA.
4 Bouvier, Geoff., (2023). *Us From Nothing: a poetic history,* Hamilton, ON.
5 petespress.ca., (2024).
6 Bruce Cockburn, "Push Come To Shove," O Sun O Moon, True North Records, 2023.

robots are making art
weird little freaks are doing all the bullshit jobs
it's all so depressingly un-hip
DUNE
THEREALFLYDOG - MMXXV

6

Choosing to leave AI behind

by Andrea Martineau

"Forced inevitability gives the patriarchal ick, artificial intelligence is for those who lack any intelligence at all," I need to yell. I truly just need to let off some steam. Shall we select a field to gather at and scream in?

Every writing break today I've taken to mindlessly scrolling, and I have been inundated with AI. News about the AI data centre that is being pushed through in Regina, Reese Witherspoon crooning about how I need to get on board with AI, yet another artist's livelihood has been ripped off by AI. It's everywhere, I can't escape it, and I despise it.

Conversations about artificial intelligence (AI) first regularly entered my life about a year or two ago when I was working as an arts administrator for a government agency.

"How are you using AI?" was added as a roundtable question to our monthly staff meeting agendas with the implication that we should be safely using AI in our workflows to improve efficiencies in some way. This puzzled me greatly. On the regular, we received disturbing updates from the creative sectors we were mandated to support about how AI was literally destroying their livelihoods and likelihood of economic success - in other words, the whole reason our agency existed. On top of that, we had uber strict privacy policies to adhere to as a government entity. And yet, despite being a staff with incredibly varied technological literacy (some of us were coding entire platforms, while some of us referred to AI as "IA" despite repeated correction), we were being instructed to go ahead and implement this technology with minimal instruction. Despite articles shared about AI mishaps, AI IP theft, and AI hallucinations, leadership went ahead with using AI to analyze data, HR went ahead with using AI to do… pretty much everything, and everyone else was left to their own devices and moral compasses. *Yikes.* It just kept being pressed upon staff as the new norm, regardless of the consequences.

My second memorable moment of rage involving AI was at a youth leadership conference (yes, at the ripe old age of 29, I was still considered a youth that summer). A presenter had been contracted to speak about utilizing AI to market your cause. He was relentless about needing to use AI in order to keep up with the times and not get left behind. "Getting left behind" seems to be the key fear-mongering phrase dude bros enjoy using most to manipulate people into using AI. Nevermind the fact that he was speaking to a socially conscious, environmentally minded audience of youth activists, and AI is devastating to the environment and working-class communities. He did not touch on that at all. He just plowed ahead, telling us we had to get on board or be left in the dust. How absolutely, stereotypically male – to force a process, an ideology, without forethought or regard for the impact it may have on literally everyone else in the world.

The forced inevitability of mass AI usage drives me up the wall. Under this category of rage, please find the sub-category of rage pertaining to the girl-bossification, faux-feminism of Reese Witherspoon et al: "C'mon ladies, we can learn together, AI isn't just for the boys, let's not get left behind!" It's very much giving the vibe "our friends are jumping off the cliff so we must too". Nah, I'm not running towards this cliff. I won't be *dragged* towards it either, thank you very much.

This forced inevitability reminds me of the wedding reception of one of my older cousins. My parents were loading up their vehicle to take myself, my grandma, my siblings, and one or two of my cousins back to the hotel we were all staying at. My cousin and I were in our first year of university, barely eighteen or nineteen at the time. My grandma giddily turned to us and said "Oh pretty soon that will be you, having your weddings next!" and it made my stomach churn. I want that? Since when? I have to do that? Says who? And *SOON*?

I feel the same way about AI. They say it's useful. Is it though? Would I get left behind? Says who, and do I give a damn about their unqualified opinion? Who decided this is the chosen path for us all? Because fuck that noise.

As a writer, non-writers or writing-adjacent professionals are always pitching AI to me to "make my work easier"

"It can help you with your edits!"

"It can help you with the tone of your emails, or to catch up on emails!"

Lord, what an insult. I spent four years in school to earn a Bachelor of Arts in English with a minor in Psychology and a certificate in Public Relations. I studied publishing! I studied entertainment law! I interned! I did so because I enjoy it. I enjoy connecting with people and deeply care about my clients. I put thought into their concerns and therefore put personal effort into my responses to them, regardless of the context. I have been writing for 25 years. I am continuously working to hone my communication skills both professionally and creatively.

I write, edit, communicate – yes, even emails, because it is my passion and my profession. To suggest that A) I should give up what I enjoy so that a water-wasting robot can do it, B) a water-wasting robot that has been proven to suck can do it better than me (or others much more experienced and qualified than me), and C) that I'm ethically accepting of a water-wasting robot that is known to steal the work of myself and my peers, IS WILDLY INSULTING.

Do these AI suggesters pick up on this, though? No. As it so happens, AI-users seem to be lacking in empathy. Now I'm not sure if this a chicken vs. egg situation, that if those who are naturally lacking in empathy are more likely to use AI or if using AI eventually leads to a lack in empathy, or, Jesus H. Christ forbid, *both.* Anecdotally and personally however, the latter seems to be my experience.

I once worked with a colleague who I did not have much in common with. They were an extroverted communications professional, I was an introverted creative. One of the few commonalities we had was that we both appreciated good writing. Her written work was concise and professional, and she was an avid reader. She was damn good at her job. Thanks to company chats and in person conversations, she was entirely up to speed on how AI was devastating the writing and publishing community: how writers I know had their books combed through without their consent in recent AI crawls, how freelancers were losing their jobs because of AI, how publishing clients were dealing with a saturated market of fake AI generated books and AI authors in the marketplace, etc. I asked for her assistance in creating speaking notes for an upcoming music conference – and she returned to me with an AI-generated speech. Despite full knowledge of the aforementioned, on top of the grievances AI has caused the music industry, she saw no issue with sending me off to that conference with an AI generated speech, and even created a "joke" version (that wasn't funny) to send me along as well for a laugh in addition to the real one. No respect for what I thought was our shared craft, no respect for our creative clients, no empathy for what any of them were going through. She's a smart person. She had the skills. And yet, she'd delegated so much to AI for no reason at all. I did not go to that conference, and I did not read that speech out loud to anyone, thankfully.

It feels a bit hopeless, sometimes. I don't know how we slow the roll of AI. How do you convince others that AI causes harm, and that that harm means you should not use it? How do you win against greedy billionaires bullying their way into developing rural land into data centres? How do we protect water and art and human soul?

I have no idea, personally. But I won't stop screaming about it, I won't stop insulting AI incels, I won't stop calling out people who use AI in dumb ways, I won't stop signing petitions and protesting, I won't stop being angry, and I won't stop being a human who writes her own goddamn emails.

Recommended Reading and References

ALSO AVAILABLE AT HTTPS://PADLET.COM/ LAURENUU/ANTIAI

Compiled by Lauren Woolsey

(Suggested starting point: # 1 generally, or # 5 for the environment. Most important to read: # 20)

1. Wolverton, Troy (2025) "Is AI Worth It?" Nob Hill Gazette https://www.nobhillgazette.com/
2. O'Donnell, James and Crownhart Casey (2024) "We did the math on AI's energy footprint. Here's the story you haven't heard" MIT Technology Review https://www.technologyreview.com/
3. International Energy Agency (2025), Energy and AI, IEA, Paris https://www.iea.org/reports/energy-and-ai

4. Verma, Pranshu and Tan, Shelly (2024) "A bottle of water per email: the hidden environmental costs of using AI chatbots" Washington Post https://www.washingtonpost.com/
5. McMenamin, Lex (2025) "ChatGPT Is Everywhere – Why Aren't We Talking About Its Environmental Costs?" Teen Vogue https://www.teenvogue.com/
6. Wittenberg, Ariel (2025) "'How come I can't breathe?': Musk's data company draws a backlash in Memphis" Politico https://www.politico.com/
7. Hall, Rachel (2025) "Heavy ChatGPT users tend to be more lonely, suggests research" The Guardian https://www.theguardian.com/
8. Klee, Miles (2025) "People Are Losing Loved Ones to AI-Fueled Spiritual Fantasies" Rolling Stone https://www.rollingstone.com/
9. Lee, Hao-Ping and Sarkar, Advait and Tankelevitch, Lev and Drosos, Ian and Rintel, Sean and Banks, Richard and Wilson, Nicholas (2025) "The Impact of Generative AI on Critical Thinking: Self-Reported Reductions in Cognitive Effort and Confidence Effects [...] of Knowledge Workers" Association for Computing Machinery, NY USA https://doi.org/10.1145/3706598.3713778
10. Marcus, Gary F. (2024) Taming Silicon Valley: How We Can Ensure That AI Works for Us, The MIT Press, ISBN: 978-0262551069
11. Waktins, Gareth (2025) "AI: The New Aesthetics of Fascism" New Socialist https://newsocialist.org.uk/
12. Haskins, Caroline (2024) "The Low-Paid Humans Behind AI's Smarts Ask Biden to Free Them From 'Modern Day Slavery'" Wired https://www.wired.com/
13. UN Trade and Development (2025) Technology and innovation report 2025 https://unctad.org/publication/technology-and-innovation-report-2025
14. McQuillan, Dan (2025) "Resisting AI: An Anti-fascist Approach to Artificial Intelligence" Bristol University Press, ISBN: 978-1529213508

15. Murphy, Hannah and Criddle, Cristina (2025) "Elon Musk's AI chatbot shared 'white genocide' tropes on X" Financial Times https://www.ft.com/
16. Davis, Jonathan (2024) Understanding Anthropic's Golden Gate Claude" Medium https://medium.com/
17. McMahon, Bryan (2025) "Bubble Trouble: An AI bubble threatens Silicon Valley, and all of us" The American Prospect https://prospect.org/ and in print
18. Brown, Mandy (2025) "Toolmen" A Working Library https://aworkinglibrary.com/writing/toolmen
19. Torres, Émile P. (2025) "The Endgame of Edgelord Eschatology" TruthDig https://www.truthdig.com/
20. Torres, Émile P. (2023) "TESCREAL: The Acronym Behind Our Wildest AI Dreams and Nightmares" TruthDig https://www.truthdig.com/

ABOUT THE AUTHORS

Annabel Townsend is a writer, entrepreneur, booklover and anthropologist at heart. She gained her PhD. from the University of Sheffield, UK before emigrating to Saskatchewan, Canada. She writes creative nonfiction and occasionally dabbles into sci-fi, and every first draft is handwritten in messy cursive. Annabel founded Pete's Press in 2024 as a means of building a community of writers and creatives, and championing the connections that form through sharing the written word.

The art in this volume was provided by **The REAL FlyDog.** He is a profligate shit-poster who lives at a fortified compound in Moose Jaw with his loving wife, six feral cats, and a cache of firearms. When he's not trying to build world communism, he obsessively collects retro advertising, Canadian Tire catalogues, and stolen fonts as the reagents to make agitprop casseroles no one asked for. He resolves to build a garden this year, because you can't eat bullets. But you can eat potatoes. In fact, you can do a lot of things with potatoes. You can boil them, mash them, even stick them into a stew....

S. Portico Bowman is an author, artist, educator and hopeful soul. Her manuscript *Would You Give Up Arms For Wings? A story inspired by the visionary life & writings of Paulus Berensohn* was chosen as one of ten finalists for the 2024 AWP Sue William Silverman Prize for Creative Nonfiction. The manuscript received generous support from the Canada Council for the Arts.

The book at its core is about overcoming creative fear and moves back and forth between membranes of reality, imagination, fiction, and non-fiction in a story that AI would never believe.

Kai Hutchence is the author behind 'The Teacher's Guide to Scratch' book series and CEO of Massive Corporation a game and educational development company. He's developed in-class and teacher training coding and AI workshops used across Canada, including a course on AI & Ethics, as well as interactive exhibits for major public venues.

Having been a game designer, app developer, author, educator, chef restaurateur, community leader and serial entrepreneur, he's guest lectured at over 20 post-secondary institutes in Education, Computer Science and Entrepreneurship and helped thousands discover the creative joy of coding.

John Klein is a friendly cyborg who lives in Regina, Saskatchewan, Treaty 4. He has an education in computer science and has worked in technology support for over three decades. His blog, *Saskboy's Abandoned Stuff* has been among the top political blogs in Canada at various times over the last two decades.

Andrea Martineau is a writer, poet, bibliophile, and phytomaniac with a penchant for heritage buildings and their paranormal tenants. She left her hometown of Moose Jaw, Saskatchewan to complete her Bachelor of Arts in English and Certificate in Public Relations at the University of Regina. Her poetry has previously been published in *untethered* magazine, *Blank Spaces, [SPACE], Figroot Press,* and *The League of Canadian Poets' Poetry Pause.* She now resides on Treaty Four Territory in oskana kâ-asastêki (Regina, Saskatchewan) with her family, rescue cats, Horsfield tortoise, and collection of houseplants, where she is writing her first novel.

www.ingramcontent.com/pod-product-compliance
Lightning Source LLC
Chambersburg PA
CBHW071358230926
51846CB00002B/585
9781997713050